MYSTERIOUS KINGSTON

BY BARBARA AND TRACY RUSSELL

Other 'mysterious' books:

Mysterious Wimbledon
More Mysterious Wimbledon

by Ruth Murphy & Clive Whichelow
(Enigma Publishing)

Published by

Twilight Books
11 Mina Road
Wimbledon
SW19 3AU

Copies of 'Mysterious Kingston' can be obtained from the publishers at the above
address for £2.95 including postage.

First edition June 1996

ISBN 0 9528524 0 3

Printed by Roebuck Press

CONTENTS

	PAGE
Introduction	5
A Disturbing Ghost on the Richmond Road	6
All Saints' - A Church with an Intriguing Past	7
The Plough Inn - An Old Haunt of Dick Turpin?	8
Maypoles and Mayhem	10
The Home of Compassion	12
Great Balls of Fire	14
A Wandering White Lady - is it Sibell Penn?	15
Cardinal Wolsey's Premonition	16
Hampton Court - A Haunted Palace	17
Things That Go Bump...	19
George Fox - Prophet and Visionary	21
The House on the Hill	22
Miracle Cures - Ancient and 'Modern'	24
A Couple of UFO Sightings	26
The Kingston Zodiac	27
The Coronation Stone - A Magical Object?	28
Curious Tales of Kingston's Kings	29
An Eerie Encounter on the Portsmouth Road	30
Is There Anybody Still There?	31

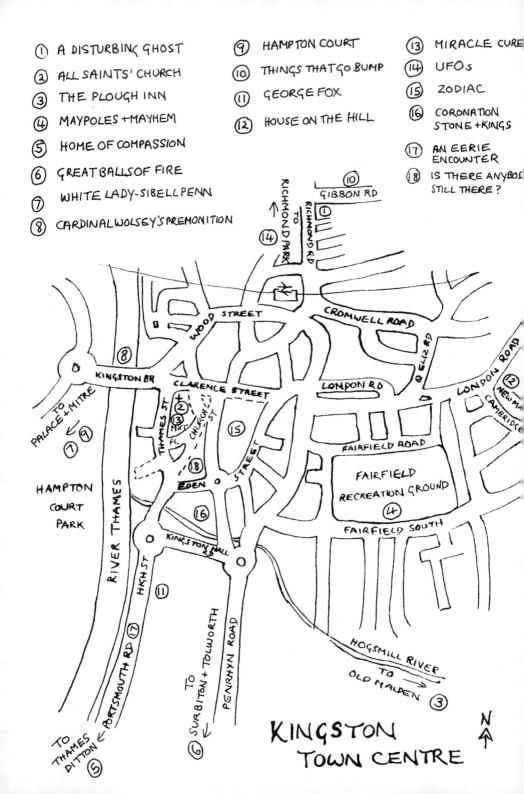

1. A DISTURBING GHOST
2. ALL SAINTS' CHURCH
3. THE PLOUGH INN
4. MAYPOLES + MAYHEM
5. HOME OF COMPASSION
6. GREAT BALLS OF FIRE
7. WHITE LADY - SIBELL PENN
8. CARDINAL WOLSEY'S PREMONITION
9. HAMPTON COURT
10. THINGS THAT GO BUMP
11. GEORGE FOX
12. HOUSE ON THE HILL
13. MIRACLE CURE
14. UFOs
15. ZODIAC
16. CORONATION STONE + KINGS
17. AN EERIE ENCOUNTER
18. IS THERE ANYBODY STILL THERE?

KINGSTON TOWN CENTRE

INTRODUCTION

Kingston has a fascinating past that stretches back more than 2,000 years, so it's hardly surprising that the area has a lot to offer the seeker after the strange and unusual. This book contains only a small sample of stories, and includes hauntings, mysteries, folklore - and anything else that doesn't quite 'fit'. There must be many more intriguing tales waiting to be discovered. If you know of any we would be very pleased to hear from you!

We have interpreted the idea of Kingston's boundaries quite freely. Boundaries are man-made, and have shifted a lot over the centuries (and are continuing to shift). We feel that this has given us the freedom to include places just outside the town's perimeters. We're sure it would be disappointing for the reader if we *didn't* include Hampton Court, for example, especially as the fortunes of Kingston and the Palace have always been closely linked. It's also hard to separate areas like Richmond Park from the town's history.

Kingston is an ancient Borough which has enjoyed Royal status for well over 1000 years. It is the oldest of the four Royal Boroughs and the smallest of all the London boroughs - though some say the most attractive!

The town's importance owes much to the river which at one time was wider and more shallow than it is now, and the first convenient fording point above the sea. Rumour claims that it was here that Julius Caesar and his invading army crossed the river in 55 BC - a crossing which led to the Roman Conquest. (Whether or not he actually *did* come to Kingston is probably one of the town's earliest mysteries!)

The Market Place is a notable landmark. A market has occupied the town centre for over 1000 years. The immediate area has, they say, the best preserved medieval street pattern in Greater London. The enigmatic Coronation Stone, on which seven Saxon kings were allegedly crowned, is another claim to fame of which the town is justly proud.

If you'd like to learn more about historic Kingston, the **Kingston Tourist Guides** can take you on guided walks throughout the year. (Contact the Kingston Tourist Information Centre at the Market House, Market Place, Kingston. Tel no: 0181 547 5592.) As it happens, one of the authors of this book (Barbara) is a town guide.

Of course, you don't have to delve too far into the past for stories; there is much evidence for spine-tingling happenings taking place today. Just look around you - if you dare...

The more adventurous investigators might like to contact **ASSAP** (The Association for the Scientific Study of Anomalous Phenomena) for support. Membership details from: Hugh Pincott, ASSAP Secretary, 20 Paul Street, Frome, Somerset, BA11 1DX.

Good hunting!

Barbara and Tracy Russell
June 1996

A DISTURBING GHOST ON THE RICHMOND ROAD

Twenty years ago, seven workmen who were converting an old Victorian house into offices threatened to go on strike. After weeks of extraordinary disruptions they felt that enough was enough.

At 82 Richmond Road, bricks flew through the air, light bulbs popped out of sockets and bottles smashed against walls. One of the workmen, Ted Marsh (pseudonym), reported that they were all convinced that a poltergeist called Albert was responsible.

The name 'Albert' had appeared on several pieces of wood including a carpenter's tool box. The carpenter was so terrified that he refused to carry on working at the house and wouldn't even touch his toolbox. The others, more bravely, were at least prepared to pick up their tools - if only to lay them down again if the situation got any worse.

A workman standing against a wall was almost strangled by a protruding electric wire. Another alleged that he was dragged across the floor by his outstretched arms, in front of witnesses. The *Surrey Comet* sent along Tom Harris (pseudonym) to investigate.

Tom wandered in through the front door, looking for someone to talk to about the many reported incidents. As he was passing the foot of the bannisters he became aware of something flying down the stairs. He turned sharply to see a piece of wood hurtling down the hall towards the front door. Peering up the stairs, it was clear that no one was there. He cautiously made his way up to the second floor where the men were working. None of them was in the least surprised to hear of Tom's close call. They were happy to show him around the building.

The brief tour passed without incident - until four of the men, including Tom, decided to go down the wooden steps to the dark, stone cellar. They stood for a moment, blinking into the gloom. Suddenly, two nails clattered to the floor. Tom looked at the others - had anyone thrown them? But he realised at once that, from where the men were standing, this was impossible. Immediately after this incident, a two-foot piece of lead pipe crashed from the wall to the floor. The pipe bounced around for several seconds before lying still. The small room became very cold, and the atmosphere tense.

At this point, they decided to clamber back to the relative safety of the ground floor area. Mr Don Stark (pseudonym), managing director of the building contractors, denied having experienced anything himself. His only concern was to get the work finished on time.

Despite Albert's intervention, the offices were eventually completed and today accommodate an estate agent's, Keith Morling. We spoke to Mr Morling in his light and airy office. He has been there since 1989 and happily has no further disturbances to report. For some reason, the launderette next door was once suggested as the focus of Albert's antics. Our enquiries confirmed that this had never been the case. Had the sight of flapping white sheets somehow confused the issue?

ALL SAINTS' - A CHURCH WITH AN INTRIGUING PAST

Situated by the Market Place, in the heart of Kingston, All Saints' Church has been a focal point of the community for centuries. In medieval times, it was also an important ecclesiastical centre; the Bishops of Winchester established a Palace nearby. The magnificent Frobenius organ was installed a few years ago; regular recitals continue to give enormous pleasure.

In days gone by, music-making was often frowned upon. In the 13th and 14th centuries, people regarded the church and the churchyard as a sort of early Leisure Centre - they sang ballads, juggled and performed 'loose dances'. William of Wykeham (the 'Bishop out of Residence') rather churlishly put a stop to all this exuberant behaviour in 1309.

Over the years, a mythology has sprung up around the church. At one time, for example, it's said that the door on the north side of the church - the one furthest from the font - was kept open during baptisms in order to 'let the Devil out'. And in 1445, the timber spire (no longer there) was struck by lightning. A pious parishoner, praying for deliverance, misinterpreted the signs: seeing the brilliant white light, he promptly 'died through fear of a spirit which he saw there'.

In 1729, the sexton, Abraham Hammerton, and his daughter Esther were digging a grave by the old St Mary's Chapel, next to the present church. Abraham accidentally struck one of the Chapel's main pillars; much of the building collapsed, killing the sexton himself and two others. Fortuitously, a pillar fell across the grave, and Esther was saved. Stories of her 'miraculous' escape spread far and wide. Emboldened, no doubt, by her narrow shave and subsequent fame, Esther threw corsets to the wind; she took to wearing men's clothing, and also took on her father's responsibilities as sexton.

A delightful story was sent to us by Mrs Olney. It was told to her by her great-great grandmother. In 1860, an old couple wanted to be buried together in All Saints' Churchyard. The husband died first, just a few days before Christmas. He was buried in the churchyard.

A few years later, his wife died. There was no more room in the churchyard, so she was buried nearby in the grounds that are now known as the Memorial Gardens. Every year, just a few days before Christmas, the husband's ghost, unhappy at being parted from his wife, walked across at night to his wife's grave. After Christmas, he left the Gardens and walked back to his grave in the churchyard...

All Saints' Churchyard was cleared over sixty years ago. We hope the couple has found other ways of keeping up their Christmas tryst.

THE PLOUGH INN - AN OLD HAUNT OF DICK TURPIN?

The report in the March 1980 edition of the *Kingston Borough News* describing a 'shadowy thing' at the Plough Inn, Old Malden, sounded rather vague and hardly worth following up. But a bitingly cold wind and a hint of sleet in the air made the thought of a pub lunch seem very inviting. The report also mentioned a 'gruesome relic' - an old skeleton, kept on the bar and regarded with affection by the regulars. That in itself, we thought, should be worth a visit.

The Plough Inn, with its blazing fire and old oak beams, is wonderfully atmospheric. Sadly, since becoming a Harvester's Inn 10 years ago, the skeleton has been removed from the bar and hidden away somewhere. But instead, working *behind* the bar, were Al and Michael. They were very helpful, and well-informed about the Inn's history.

They had no idea of the skeleton's former identity: they only knew that it had been found in a secret passage at the Inn. We mentioned that a former manageress had felt that, late at night, the skeleton had 'seemed to have company'. She had often been aware of a black shape, standing in the doorway, that disappeared 'just as you turned round'. Her husband, however, had dismissed all this as 'just her imagination'.

Al and Michael had heard vague talk of ghosts, but said that nothing much was happening nowadays. Of course, they said, you could never tell with ghosts - there were times when glasses would mysteriously fall off the top shelf, despite being placed quite far back. And a manager had once stacked up a pile of pans, only to have it collapse shortly after. 'Glasses and pans ought to fall down straight away, not an hour later,' said the barmen.

Parts of The Plough date back about 500 years. One of the most intriguing aspects of its long history is the alleged association with Dick Turpin. (There's no real evidence to link him with the shadowy ghost, although, 'He *could* be,' said Al.)

A small room by the bar is called 'Dick Turpin's Room'. In a recess by the fireplace was the entrance to a secret stairway (now bricked up), which led to a room without windows. Here, plans could be laid without fear of being seen or disturbed.

We could picture the scene... Dick Turpin evading the Bow Street Runners, dashing across the green in front of the Inn, up the stairway to the secret room to stash away the spoils, waiting until the coast was clear to creep down an escape hatch behind the chimney to his waiting horse, and making his getaway...

According to a report in a 1928 copy of the *Malden Gazette* (kept tucked away behind the bar), there is something 'deeper and more mystical' about the secret stairway. The account says it must have been actually built into the house, as it had been 'specially bricked', and tells us that the innkeeper must have had it built during the 'troublous times of Charles 1, or during the Commonwealth'. The writer adds: 'For what or for whom? For romance or tragedy?' We'll probably never know.

Our later research revealed that bomb damage in 1944 had led to the discovery of a secret room hidden in the roofs of cottages nos. 28 and 30 Church Road, opposite the Plough. The cottages, believed to have been originally one single cottage, form part of a group of dwelling houses thought to date from the 18th century. A romantic idea that the secret room was once linked to the Plough by a tunnel has not yet, unfortunately, been substantiated.

But if it's the ghost of a highwayman you're looking for, a better bet might be the shade of the notorious Jerry Abershawe. Born in Kingston in 1773, 30 years after Dick Turpin's death, he is also said to have been a regular at the Plough. But his spectral presence is seen not at the Inn, but galloping across Wimbledon Common on a ghostly horse...

Al and Mike also gave us a couple of intriguing ghost stories, both of which we've used in this book.

It was a good lunch, too.

MAYPOLES AND MAYHEM

Kingstonians have always known how to have a good time even if, now and again, a reveller does get a bit carried away - sometimes literally, having jumped into the river clutching a football. On Shrove Tuesday the 'Pancake Bell' would ring out at 11 o'clock and all the apprentices in the town then assembled for a rowdy game of football. The ball was usually kept between Thames Street and the Anglers Hotel in the Portsmouth Road - unless some rascal made off with it and headed towards the river...

It's said that the Game celebrated more than just a wild fling before the lean days of Lent. It may have marked the anniversary of the Danish massacre. The people of Kingston had united in a titanic struggle against the marauding Danes until help arrived from London. Victorious, the captain's head was kicked from one man to another all around the town.

Women stayed on the sidelines unless one of them was given the honour of starting the game by throwing the ball down from the Town Hall balcony. Business was brisk in the local hostelries, and publicans often bribed the players to kick the ball in their direction. Eventually, the horseplay became very rough with bags of flour and soot being tossed into the crowd. In 1867 police reinforcements were drafted into the town and the authorities blew the whistle on the fun and games for the last time.

Fortunately, football could be played daily on the Fairfield's twenty acres, a popular playground for all kinds of activity. Once, medieval pageants were held there, as well as regular cockfighting and jousting events. The nearby water pump (now covered by a car park) was a good place for a gossip whilst filling up your bucket. Several fairs provided opportunities for high jinks. At least three were held every year: during Whitsun, Lammas (August) and the Great Allhallowtide fair which lasted seven days in its heyday. (Today's Green Fairs and May Merries seem modest affairs in comparison.)

The annual highlight was the Kyngham Games, a series of plays and dances performed during the Tudor period. They became so popular that other parishes held similar events. The Museum has a commemorative window, designed by Dr Finny in 1911, showing some of the colourful characters who took part, such as the King and Queen of May.

The Churchwardens' Accounts for 1509 contain the earliest known references to the Morris Dance and characters of the Robin Hood Games, held at Whitsun. Maid Marian, Friar Tuck and the other outlaws were able to show off their archery skills, led by Robin. All the Games were run by parish officers who paid the expenses and then collected donations in 'gaderyngs'. Any profit went towards repairs of All Saints' Church.

The Church frowned upon May merrymaking, and so missed out on some useful revenue. All maypoles were banned during the Reformation. A later revival ensured that maypoles were carried through the Market Place and then danced around in the Apple Market.

Hocktide (the second Tuesday after Easter) helped to swell the church coffers. The spirited townswomen used to throw ropes over the men and not release them until they had stumped up a contribution to the Church. The men got their own back, but demanded kisses instead of money - much to the dismay of the Church, no doubt.

The Church has enjoyed some lighthearted moments. The ancient custom of Cracknut Sunday was practised until the 18th century. The congregation used to crack nuts during Divine Service on the Sunday before Michaelmas. The din was often loud enough for the minister to break off his sermon until silence was restored. It is thought that the practice originated from the civic feast that followed the annual election of Bailiffs and Corporation on Michaelmas Day. The custom may well be pagan in origin, expressing the idea that the nut's kernel symbolises new life within the husk of Autumn.

The King of May

Until around the turn of the century, men from the farming communities would go to All Saints' Church wearing smocks. This might seem surprisingly casual wear for Divine Service, but the idea that a smock was just a simple garment worn by farm workers is misleading. The smock dates back centuries - even the word (meaning 'shift', or 'chemise') is of Anglo-Saxon origin. Men wore their Sunday best smocks with pride. They were made of best white linen - which could cost as much as two weeks' wages - and were often handed down from father to son. Lovingly embroidered by their wives, the trade of the wearer was sometimes depicted in decorated boxes (cartwheels, or crooks, for example) at the side of the smocking. You could say that the smock is a more traditional style of menswear than the bowler hat and pin-striped suit!

The ancient ceremony of 'beating the bounds' has all but died out, apart from the occasional nostalgic revival in rural parts of England. This marking-out of the parish boundaries dates from pre-Christian times, and possibly has links with paganism. Boundaries were followed precisely; good-natured parishioners were expected to open their front doors to the revellers and allow them to clamber out of a side window! The 'beating' at various points on the boundary often involved choir boys; the 'processioners' would give them a gentle, symbolic tap on the bottom with a staff. The boys were sometimes rewarded with a small gift. The boundaries between Ham and Kingston were beaten regularly until 1862, and possibly later. Men had to row down the River Thames and, if there were no boat available to cross the Penn Ponds in Richmond Park, someone had to swim across!

THE HOME OF COMPASSION

The first mention of a property on the site of the present Home in Thames Ditton appears in the Domesday Book of 1086; since then, the building has had a long and chequered history. In Erasmus Forde's time it was a large house known as Forde's Farm. After Forde's death in 1533, Henry VIII converted the whole area into a hunting ground. In the late 18th century, Charlotte Boyle took over the house. She created a splendid estate with pleasure grounds and orchards and renamed it Boyle Farm. The house then changed hands several times and in 1905 became a nursing home for elderly people run by the Sisters of Compassion, a nursing order of Benedictine nuns.

We met the director, Don Walker, who very kindly gave us a guided tour of the Home and pointed out the areas of interest. Many stories have become legend, but more recent reports suggest that people are still experiencing strange phenomena.

In the late 1970s, Derek Potts, who later became a church warden, had an encounter with a ghostly nun. He was attending a meeting at the Home and happened to mention to someone that he had never seen the chapel. He was told it was well worth a visit.

When he got to the chapel, the door opened and a nun came out. Placing her finger to her lips she silently motioned him to stay away. Later, his colleague asked him what he thought of the chapel. He explained that the nun had not allowed him to go in. His colleague looked surprised and told him that there hadn't been a nun at the Home for over a year. The last nun had died in 1976.

A former employee, Elizabeth Gadd, had a more recent experience, shortly after joining the staff in February 1990. She was going to get the supper things from the kitchen when in a nearby passage she saw a nun dressed in white and grey. Although the apparition's face was indistinct, her hands were well-defined and solid. Elizabeth hurried into the kitchen and picked up a tray; as she was coming out, she heard a sound behind her. Startled, she spun round. A figure was moving towards her. Elizabeth threw the supper things into the servery lift and darted back into the kitchen. Emerging cautiously a few minutes later, she had the disturbing sensation of the nun walking straight through her.

Linda Silver, a cleaner at the home, told us about her sighting of an odd shape in 1994. Like Elizabeth Gadd, she had also been on her way to the kitchen: 'I was going to get some supper things when I saw a grey shape like a mist going like - that..' Linda moved her arm to describe an undulating movement. She watched the shape travel from the kitchen, across the end of the passage and then enter the cook's sitting room. She was terrified. It is interesting to note that this was the same passage where Elizabeth Gadd had been taken unawares, *and* at the same time of day. And none of these witnesses were aware that the Sisters had worn white and grey habits as very few pictures of them exist.

Don told us that he once thought he saw someone sitting in a chair in the cook's sitting room. 'I came back later and someone was still sitting there - but I think it was just a shadow. Pure imagination.' Perhaps, when a place has this kind of reputation it's easy to think that your mind is playing tricks on you. Or just more reassuring.

According to Peter Underwood in *A Gazetteer of British Ghosts*, more than one Mother Superior has been convinced that a White Lady has visited her whilst she lay tucked up in bed. Don pointed out the room that had probably been the scene of these hauntings; intriguingly, it was close to the sitting room and the ghostly corridor.

Many years ago, the new Mother Superior came upon the room, which was locked at the time. She asked if it could be opened. Inside, she found it quite charming and determined to make it her bedroom. On her first night in the room, she was alarmed to see a white lady take shape in front of her. The apparition inspired such terror that she refused to spend another night there. It was locked again for several years and the story forgotten - until another Mother Superior was also intrigued by the locked room. It was opened again - and, with great delight, the nun turned it into her bedroom. That night, the ghostly white lady appeared to her. After her initial shock, she decided the presence was harmless, and even comforting! She continued to sleep there until her death, when the room was promptly locked up again.

There have been no reported sightings since. Don assured us that today the room is used just as a store room and the occasional sitting room. Unfortunately, it was locked at the time of our visit. Well, you can't be too careful...

Another resident phantom at the Home is a black dog which tends to settle on patients' beds at night, unseen by the nurses. But the dog seems to be a bad omen as patients are known to die soon afterwards. Don had heard a vague account recently of someone claiming to have seen it, but otherwise, he had no first-hand reports to tell us about.

The grounds, too, have not been without incident: a night nurse claims she once heard the sounds of children laughing in the garden, and another witness alleges he felt strongly that someone was watching him while he tended the flower beds. A policeman was once murdered on the estate; could he still be keeping a watchful eye on things?

We had a fascinating visit and are very grateful to Don Walker and the staff for giving us so much of their time. Despite the history of hauntings, the Home is welcoming and peaceful. We hope it remains so.

GREAT BALLS OF FIRE

Footballs that shatter your windows are one thing; balls of fire that hurtle into your living room when you're watching TV are quite another...

According to a report in the 31 August 1977 edition of the *Surrey Comet,* this is just what happened to Mr and Mrs Kent (pseudonyms), who were living at the time in Hook Rise South, Tolworth.

The fireball, bursting in through a side window behind the TV set, announced its presence with a loud BANG. It seems that the aerial had attracted the lightning and conducted it along the gutter and down the drainpipe. It all happened very suddenly; the Kents hadn't even realised that a storm was raging *outside*, let alone in their living room!

The effects were devastating: electrical sockets were fused, the telephones were disconnected, sulphur fumes and soot were blown down the chimney, and TV sets - not just the Kents', but others in the road - stopped working. The fireball was described as a 'huge, mauve-coloured ball that was too bright to look at'. Alarmed neighbours saw a 'sort of red glow, surrounded by smoke'.

Experts from the *Surrey Comet* said the Kents' description of the fireball incident was very similar to other accounts. But so far, no-one has come up with an adequate explanation for these (fortunately very rare) episodes of ball lightning.

Beasts like the Surrey Puma now vie with the Loch Ness Monster for pride of place in the annals of mythical beasts. The elusiveness of Nessie continues to confound researchers, but evidence is growing that real, solid 'big cats' really are prowling around the countryside. They're not a modern phenomenon: an early - and possibly the first - recorded observation of a strange beast comes from William Cobbett, author of 'Rural Rides', in 1770. As a built-up area, Kingston isn't particularly noted for big cat sightings. (There have been a few close by in the St George's area of Weybridge.) However, about six years ago, there were reports of a puma-type animal seen in Park Road, fairly near to the centre of Kingston.

A WANDERING WHITE LADY - IS IT SIBELL PENN?

A White Lady who haunts a corridor in a chilly wine cellar? This intriguing report from the *Richmond and Twickenham Informer*, November 1995, caught our attention.

The Mitre Hotel, where the Lady is said to walk, is just across the road from Hampton Court Palace. We spoke to Dawn Tomazou, who has worked at the Hotel for 25 years. She could remember several people who, over the years, had encountered the apparition. Some builders, for example, who were downstairs renovating a fireplace a few years ago, announced one day: 'We're not going down there again!' Dawn herself finds the basement area unnaturally chilly and creepy. A photographer recently tried to take some inside shots in the basement area: the flash lead exploded.

Since extensive refurbishments were completed in 1991, the apparition in the long white frock seems to have disappeared - temporarily, at least. It's just the *feeling* of a presence that's still there...

The most intriguing thing about the White Lady is that she's said to resemble strongly a phantom seen wandering in the grounds of Hampton Court. There's a theory that the corridor in the wine cellar was once part of a secret tunnel that linked the Mitre with Hampton Court. This could, it's said, have provided a 'channel' for the White Lady to use. (And would explain why there are no reports of wispy phantoms crossing the busy A308!) But who is this white-robed figure? Witnesses have suggested three possibilities: Jane Seymour and Katherine Howard (Henry VIII's 3rd and 5th wives respectively), and Sibell Penn, foster-mother to the sickly Edward VI.

Sibell Penn is perhaps the most likely candidate; she has also been spotted occasionally in nearby Hampton, and her appearance seems to fit most reports quite closely. (Although it has to be said that some witnesses describe Sibell's dress as 'grey' rather than white.) Sibell died of smallpox in 1562. Her mortal remains were interred in the old St Mary's Churchyard, her splendid tomb adorned with a full-length effigy.

But apart from an alleged sighting by Queen Elizabeth I (another former charge of Sibell Penn), Sibell's regular appearances didn't begin until 1828; her tomb was damaged when the old church, struck by lightning, was demolished. A new church was built, in an idyllic spot at the corner of Church Street and Thames Street, and the tomb was moved to the safety of the chancel. But Sibell obviously couldn't settle down in her pleasant new surroundings. She began her wanderings, enjoying particularly the occasional visit to her old rooms and spinning wheel at Hampton Court.

In 1885, curiosity got the better of the Reverend Merewether, curate at St Mary's. He enlisted the help of a church warden to investigate the contents of Sibell's tomb. Creeping into the chancel late one night, the intrepid (or *reckless*) researchers were alarmed to hear the sound of low moaning coming from the tomb. Shaking violently, the curate dropped his lantern, which promptly went out. In the darkness, an unearthly glow appeared and slowly spread over the tomb. The form of Sibell Penn, recumbent for over 250 years, was now sitting up and sobbing pitifully...

Mindful of the tradition in Hampton that the village would suffer decline and misfortune should anyone tamper with Sibell's remains, the tomb was wisely removed to the safety of the crypt. Today, Sibell rests (peacefully, we hope) in her tomb in the south-west porch of St Mary's church. Some say that Sibell Penn is the most well-authenticated 'ghost' of all time. We doubt if we've heard the last of her...

CARDINAL WOLSEY'S PREMONITION...

Looking at pictures of the rickety structure that served as Kingston's Bridge for over 700 years, it's surprising that anyone ever dared set foot on it. Nevertheless, myriads of carriages, pedestrians, beasts and their burdens *did* make their way across the bridge in relative safety. But one person probably *never* crossed over the bridge into Kingston - and that was Cardinal Wolsey...

His reluctance had nothing to do with qualms about the fragile nature of the bridge. The Cardinal was deeply superstitious about Kingston - even the very word struck terror into his heart. The road through Kingston was the most direct route from London to Hampton Court but Wolsey would choose to make a detour or travel by river.

As he lay dying in Leicester, an envoy from Henry VIII came to escort him to the Tower of London. 'What is your name, Constable?' asked Wolsey. 'My name, sire, is - *Constable Kingston*.' Wolsey sighed heavily, and died shortly after the encounter.
It's possible that this odd coincidence (*was* it a coincidence?) helped to hasten his death. If so, he was at least spared further anguish and humiliation.

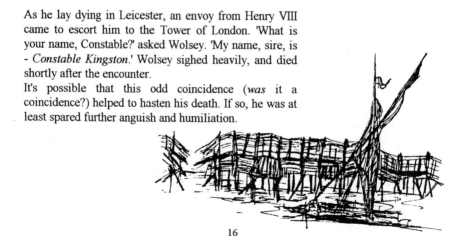

HAMPTON COURT - A HAUNTED PALACE

Whisper the word 'Macbeth' at your peril...

In true theatrical tradition, the first steward we spoke to at the Palace prudently referred to Shakespeare's darkest tragedy as 'The Scottish Play'. It's said that Shakespeare - less prudently - used the words of genuine black magic incantations in the witches' scenes, which is possibly why the play is now thought of as 'cursed'.

Written in 1606, the first performance of the play took place in the Great Watching Chamber at Hampton Court in the presence of James I. James was an obsessive king, with a passion for witchcraft - an enthusiasm that Shakepeare would probably have borne in mind when he was writing the play. But almost at once, the curse took effect... The actor playing Lady Macbeth was taken violently ill; according to some accounts, Shakespeare himself had to take over the part.

A recent visitor refused to go into the Watching Chamber as 'there was something evil in it'. The somewhat eerie atmosphere in the Chamber might be due in part to the Abraham Tapestries: woven with brilliant gold and silver threads, they are now fading. 'They look just like ghosts,' observed the steward.

Perhaps Shakespeare's untimely words are not the only reason for the unusual degree of supernatural activity at the Palace. John Chalcraft, a steward who was stoking up the log fire in the Tudor kitchens when we spoke to him, said we were 'now standing on a monks' ancient burial ground'. In the 16th century, the monks became dispossessed of their wealth and properties by Henry VIII. They became very bitter. And they cursed the new landowners in no uncertain terms. It seems inconceivable - but *could* medieval curses still affect us today?

John, a down-to-earth sort of person, told us of an odd experience he'd had in January, 1995. While stoking up the fire at about 11 o'clock in the morning, as usual, something compelled him to look through the archway that led to another part of the kitchen. Through the wall came a misty, grey disc; it was hard-edged and about 18 inches in diameter. It sailed through the entrance, drifted across the kitchen, and disappeared through another archway. John thought it was a trick of the light, but a couple of days later, the same thing happened again. Later, he heard that at least one other steward had experienced a similar 'vision'.

On another occasion, John was standing by the fireplace when he felt something solid come down on his head. It was like a hat, or a ring. 'Blimey, what the heck's that?' he thought. His colleague at the time, standing on the other side of the fireplace, said he could see a 'ring of light' around John's head. We joked about a 'slipped halo' - were the monks trying to tell him something?!

John told us about a custodian at the Palace, who used to patrol the kitchens at night. He once thought he saw a little boy turning the roasting-spit by the fire - which is just what young boys used to be employed to do.

A grace-and-favour residence above the Cumberland Suite is reputed to be haunted by a figure wearing a blue cloak. This gentleman has been sighted several times in recent years, but no-one seems to know who he is. The appartment was recently occupied by Mr and Mrs Baker and their son Mark (pseudonyms). They invited Mark's girlfriend, Lisa, to dinner. Knowing nothing of the blue-cloaked figure, she was startled to see an apparition floating past the open door. 'You've seen something, haven't you?' said Mrs Baker, noticing the odd expression on Lisa's face. Lisa described accurately the resident ghost.

Intriguingly, this ghost seems to bear a strong resemblance to the cloaked 'Sandeman Port' figure that we heard about from the Information Officer. Known also as 'The Ferryman', this spectral being appears at the West Gate of the Palace. Tradition has it that he had a tryst with an aristocatic lady who failed to turn up; possibly, she was killed. The Ferryman committed suicide.

But undoubtedly, in a building that accommodates up to 25 apparitions, it's the ghosts of Katherine Howard and Sibell Penn that vie for centre stage. In death, as in life, they are vastly different characters - although both are *heard* rather more often than seen. In the case of Katherine, some can hear her anguished screams as she hurtles along the Haunted Gallery, still pleading for a last-minute reprieve from her husband, Henry VIII. (Forget the doubters who point out that the Haunted Gallery would have been locked in Katherine's day - are ghosts deterred by mortal refinements like locks and keys?)

Sibell Penn presents a much less highly-strung image. Foster-mother to Edward VI, she was well-loved by the reserved, sickly young king. Sibell's whirring spinning wheel was heard even before she herself put in an appearance. The wheel was eventually found, gathering dust and cobwebs, behind a brick wall at the Palace. Sibell is still spotted occasionally, wandering through the Palace grounds (and possibly at the Mitre, as we've mentioned), dressed in a long grey dress and grey bonnet.

Don't restrict your visits to Hampton Court to long, hot summer days. When there's a chill in the air, and the wind whips along theTudor passageways, the stewards will have more time to tell you about the footsteps that tread heavily behind them on the ancient flagstones, and the shapes that appear in the corner of the eye that disappear as soon as you turn your head...

They can remind you that the Astronomical Clock stopped in 1619 when Queen Anne of Denmark (wife of James I) died. Legend has it that it continues its sombre warnings of death to this day. And they can tell you about hauntings that began more recently, such as the shade of Lady Gale, who died in the fire of 1986. Her face has been seen at the window of the appartment where she lived.

A word of warning...take care of all cameras and recording equipment. The recorder *we* used mangled our interview tapes as soon as we tried to play them back. This failure of mechanical apparatus seems to be a fairly common experience when investigating the paranormal.

THINGS THAT GO BUMP...

A few years ago, the Kingston guide book mentioned 'Chalky' as one of the town's attractions. Chalky was, apparently, a poltergeist at the Reject Shop (the old Empire Theatre) in Clarence Street. He used to make things fall off shelves, which must have been very inconvenient as the shop sold pottery and glassware.

Checking up on Chalky's recent activities - if any - a few weeks ago, the manageress of the Reject Shop said she had experienced nothing unusual at all. In any case, she said, the shop was about to vacate the premises and a brewery was taking over - which would, perhaps, be a more comfortable environment for spirits? But it's unlikely that Chalky will reappear, as poltergeists tend to attach themselves to people rather than places.

Poltergeists are said to be more active when there's a young child or a teenager in the house. But Peter Underwood, an experienced researcher, says that older people can also be a source of this type of psychokinetic energy. In *The Ghost Hunter's Guide* he discusses a case in Ham: an elderly lady was unable to keep any watches or clocks in her room as they mysteriously stopped working in her presence.

Hampton Court is *the* venue for typical poltergeist pranks. Most reports come from tenants of the grace-and-favour appartments in the area of Fish Court, an atmospheric backwater near the Tudor kitchens. This ancient spot is said to be 'riddled with ghosts'.

A steward told us about his Aunt, who had lived in a basement appartment in Tennis Court Lane (near Fish Court) for over sixty years. According to her, they'd never had ghosts until the 'tapestry people' came along. These 'people' were renovators whose brief was to hang full tapestries, which involved putting in support beams across the ceiling. What with all the 'banging around and everything else', Auntie felt that spirits from other parts of the Palace had been driven into her own appartment. (Few *young* people here, either.)

The renovations completed, she started losing things. Her possessions would turn up later in 'totally unexpected' places. A common experience, of course - except that in this case all Auntie's neighbours were experiencing the same sort of thing. They still are...

Perhaps the most curious poltergeist phenomenon is - puddles. A family in Gibbon Road, Kingston, was nonplussed when puddles of plain water started appearing regularly on the stone floor of their small utility room. A naturally 'wet' area, it was easy at first to put all this dampness down to leakages from the washing machine, or drips of water from the fridge door. But when they realised that drips and leakages from the appliances couldn't possibly form puddles in the *centre* of the room, they got a bit worried.

It's said that 'poltergeist puddles' have a hard, definite edge to them. The Gibbon Road family wasn't sure about edges; all they wanted to know was whether to call in the plumber or the exorcist...

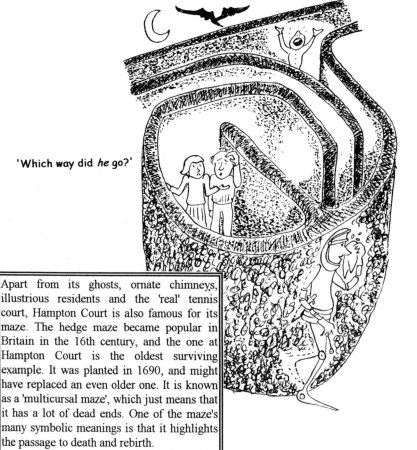

'Which way did *he* go?'

Apart from its ghosts, ornate chimneys, illustrious residents and the 'real' tennis court, Hampton Court is also famous for its maze. The hedge maze became popular in Britain in the 16th century, and the one at Hampton Court is the oldest surviving example. It was planted in 1690, and might have replaced an even older one. It is known as a 'multicursal maze', which just means that it has a lot of dead ends. One of the maze's many symbolic meanings is that it highlights the passage to death and rebirth.

GEORGE FOX - PROPHET AND VISIONARY

Kingston has a long history of non-conformity; preachers have been put to death for their radical views. The founder of the Society of Friends, George Fox, came to preach in Kingston many times; despite the risks to his followers, his meetings at the building once known as the King John's Dairy (no longer there) in the High Street were well-attended.

George Fox was born in 1624 during very troubled political and religious times. He believed that by practising silent contemplation it was possible to follow an inward light and find personal direction. At meetings, people sat quietly until the intensity of worship would move them to shake and quiver, which gave rise to the movement's name of 'Quakers'. George was even known to 'shake' the building on occasion. He was also capable of lengthy trances, and endured one particular trance for a total of fourteen days.

His striking looks and personality attracted many disciples. He demonstrated miraculous powers of healing which helped to establish his reputation. A man with a dislocated neck recovered after just a few moments with George. Another lay in agony with an injured arm and was instantly healed by him.

He also attracted a good many enemies amongst the clergy and was regularly put in the stocks or imprisoned. After a fierce beating, he was accused of being in league with the Devil when his assailants failed to draw blood. Once, he rode over quicksands, and swam with his horse through treacherous waters without realising the dangers. The locals could not believe he had escaped drowning and proclaimed him a witch.

George stood alone in condemning the madness of witch-hunts, which only confirmed people's suspicions of him. Quakers often found themselves on trumped-up charges and had to stand trial. One woman accused two Quakers of bewitching her. She claimed that during the night as she lay asleep, she was transformed into a mare and ridden to a meeting. She showed the marks of spurs and bruises to magistrates. On this occasion, common sense prevailed and the prisoners were found not guilty.

George did not help his cause by claiming to have visions on Pendle Hill, an area notorious for its association with witches. Gazing over Wensleydale from the hill, he had a vision of a group of people dressed in white. They later became his first congregation.

Not everyone took a dim view of George's visions. Oliver Cromwell was grateful to George for several helpful prophecies, including the prediction that he would never take the office or title of King. In 1658, the two men arranged a meeting at Hampton Court. As George watched Cromwell riding into Hampton Court Park, he claims, 'I saw and felt a waft of death go forth against him, and when I came to him he looked like a dead man'. Cromwell died soon afterwards.

Other visions included the fall of the Rump Parliament and the Great Fire of London. Unfortunately, as witchcraft hysteria increased, he paid the price for his extraordinary abilities with public scorn and frequent imprisonment. Nevertheless, there is no doubt that George Fox was a visionary with remarkable healing and clairvoyant powers.

THE HOUSE ON THE HILL

When the estate agent's details emphasised the 'original features' of the house in New Malden, the Potters weren't expecting the former occupants to be still in residence. On viewing the property, the family was tempted by the peaceful location on the hill and the reasonable asking price. They gladly snapped it up. The house had been standing empty for some years when Mr and Mrs Potter and their four children moved there in 1971.

It was in desperate need of modernisation, but this was part of the attraction of the house. The dark hallway, the sunken rose garden, the tendrils of wisteria clinging to the posts of the terrace all added to a feeling that time had stood still. The house deeds indicated that at one time the house had offered convalescence to patients with tuberculosis. The french windows opened onto a sunlit terrace that had a 1935 Factory Acts thermometer still swinging from its roof. Caught up in the atmosphere of gloom and decay, perhaps it's no wonder that the family experienced some phenomena that they couldn't readily explain.

As the removal van drew up on the first day a glass lamp, previously hanging in the porch, was found lying unbroken on the tiled doorstep. It was replaced without further incident until the morning the family left seven years later. Once again the lamp was discovered on the doorstep, quite undamaged.

There seem to have been several sightings of a man in period dress possibly from the twenties. Gina, who was seven at the time, was in the garden early one spring morning when she became aware of a rather handsome gentleman in his thirties, standing on the path. He was looking at her and smiling while doing up his collar shirt buttons. She remembers his dark, greased-back hair and that he was sporting neat cuffs, high waisted black trousers and very shiny shoes. She was too astonished to speak and after a few moments the image disappeared. She told no one about it. A couple of weeks later, Gina's nine year old sister Sally reported seeing a man answering the same description, doing up his shirt buttons, in her parents' bedroom. Indeed, Mrs Potter saw a tall, dark man standing at the foot of the bed one night. Once, at about midnight, she recalls hearing a child's voice calling 'mother' outside the door and, on taking a look, found no one there.

The children seemed to find this room threatening and would run swiftly past the open door en route to the bathroom. To relieve the sombre air of the upstairs landing, the Potters decided to brighten things up with all-the-rage purple and turquoise. They were all happy with the new decor but somehow the atmosphere seemed no lighter than before. Perhaps prints in the menacing style of Aubrey Beardsley hadn't been such a good idea.

Children can be impressionable, but perhaps grown-ups are too. Mr Potter recalls looking out of the bedroom window one morning to see a ruddy-cheeked boy standing in the rose garden. Nothing odd about that, especially with a couple of teenage girls in the house, but this young chap was dressed in pre-war school uniform. He beamed up at Mr Potter cheerfully before vanishing.

So far, none of these experiences suggests the residents of a convalescent home. A possible reminder is the appearance of a slender female hand that emerged from behind the partly opened living room door; the wispy hand passed over a light switch before withdrawing behind the door again. It was late evening, and Sally was standing in the middle of the room, chatting to her parents; she stopped in mid-flow as she witnessed the extraordinary sight. What makes it more interesting is that eighteen months earlier she had stumbled into her parents' room one night in a trance-like state and exhorted them to switch off the light. Her puzzled parents were having none of it as they attempted to carry on reading and after a while she wandered back to bed. The next morning, she declared she had no recollection of her visit at all. Was this the spirit of a very thrifty housekeeper still making itself known? Or a nurse intent on everyone getting a good night's sleep?

Animals are known to be sensitive to atmosphere and the family cat was no exception. Hattie, a tortoiseshell, had been the sole survivor of a rubbish tip dumping - possibly protected, the family felt, by the marked yellow cross on her front. According to Mrs Potter, the cat had a habit of turning up in a room when the door was closed - as though she could walk through walls. One day, she walked away and was never seen again.

Today, each member of the family still has vivid memories of living in the house - even if Dad does need prompting that, yes, he did claim to see a cowled figure crouching outside the kitchen door, and they have to take Mum's word that light bulbs used to leap out of lamps for no apparent reason and that door handles would turn with nobody behind them. Bobby, ten at the time, recalls the family's last day. Strangely, all the clinging wisteria had disentangled itself from the posts and was lying limply across the terrace floor.

It's now nearly twenty years since the Potters left the house but they're still in touch with their old next door neighbour. This neighbour soon became quite friendly with the family that moved in afterwards. She recalls a conversation that she had with the twelve year old daughter, shortly after their arrival. Chatting over the garden fence, she enquired how they were all settling in and so on. The girl looked at her seriously for a moment. 'Do you believe in ghosts?' she asked. The neighbour said 'no', and smiled reassuringly...

Nothing too alarming can have disturbed the family as they're still living there today. Since they extensively modernised the house (an undertaking which is supposed to either 'exorcise' spirits or spark them into action), no one likes to ask if they have experienced any further manifestations. Somehow, it would be disappointing to hear that they hadn't.

It's good to hear of spirits who have a grasp of modern technology. A school, just outside the Kingston boundaries, incorporates in its grounds a Victorian house that once belonged to an influential gentleman. A few years ago the caretaker, Tony (pseudonym), said he found the house eerie and unwelcoming. He kept one particular room locked - and no amount of cajoling would induce him to produce the key. It was the faces that kept appearing at the window that put him off. Oddly enough, Tony seemed to feel more at home in the room used as an office. Or the room that *had* been used as an office - until the day a secretary walked in and saw a message on her (switched off) computer that read: **COME OVER HERE**...
She didn't - she ran out of the room...

MIRACLE CURES - ANCIENT AND 'MODERN'

Thinking of areas associated with miraculous healing, Kingston probably isn't the first place that springs to mind.

To some extent, that might be Kingston's own fault. Mary Caine, author of *The Kingston Zodiac,* regards the area we now know as Seething Wells as a 'magical', prehistoric healing centre. Biden, the 16th century local historian, also mentions these natural springs in his *History of Kingston.* Apart from the general medicinal properties of the hot wells, the waters were considered particularly beneficial for eye problems.

So what went wrong? Unlike the soothing springs of other early settlements, such as Bath, those at Kingston have disappeared, their benefits unappreciated. Cardinal Wolsey believed that the waters from Coombe Springs could ease kidney stones. He had the waters piped to Hampton Court, three and a half miles away.

But Kingston isn't short of *people* who have been credited with miraculous healing powers. There was St Blaise, for example. Martyred in the 4th century AD, he was the patron saint of woollen drapers, a guild that flourished in Kingston in medieval times. A picture of him, holding his woolcomb, hangs in All Saints' Church. St Blaise intercedes in cases of diseases affecting cattle, and of the throat; it's said that, in life, he miraculously cured a young child who was choking to death on a fish-bone.

St Blaise was a teacher as well as a healer. According to the legend of the Holy Grail, he taught Merlin, the magician. And he actually made King Arthur's Round Table.

There was a thriving trade in 'miracle cures' in Kingston in the 19th century. Given the powerful effect of mind over matter, some of these potions might even have have worked. In 1890, a North American Indian Chief called Sequah turned up in Kingston Market Place, his scarlet and gold carriage laden with miraculous remedies from the prairies.

The townsfolk flocked to him in droves. From his pitch outside the Griffin Hotel, Sequah dispensed 'secret' potions to cure all ailments from digestive disorders to paralysis. Even the discovery that there were 23 other 'Sequahs' operating all over England failed to diminish the people's enthusiasm for his quack cures.

In the absence of effective, tested medicines, these rather dubious healers acquired some illustrious supporters. There was the Duchess of Kent (the mother of Queen Victoria), for example; she was a great advocate of the remedies of Edward Phillips.

Unlike the unscrupulous Sequah, Phillips seems to have been a popular, kind-hearted man. He brewed his concoctions in the kitchen of his home at no. 20 Thames Street. Demand exceeded supply for his 'Cordial Aperient Draught' during the cholera epidemic of 1854. A Mr Geach swore he'd saved a man's life by giving him a dose of Phillips's secret recipe.

We are indebted to Winnie Stewart for her reminiscences. Winnie recalls her (surprisingly recent) days as a stall-holder in Kingston's Monday Cattle Market. Mothers, she says, seeing a gypsy leading a horse, would give a bit of silver (usually a threepenny bit) for a horse hair to cure their children's warts. The hair would be wound round the wart until it dropped off. On a nearby stall, there was a 'noisy quack doctor who sold brightly coloured medicine as a cure for everything'.

Winnie certainly has some intriguing acquaintances: one, for example, can remember the days when roasted mice were eaten as a cure for bronchitis! Winnie's husband, a pilot, was often asked to fly people in his aeroplane as a cure for the same complaint. Another suggested 'peeing over chilblains after drinking Guiness' ,which was an old Irish cure! (Were some diseases preferable to the treatment?)

A report in the *Kingston Borough News*, October 1977, mentions a phenomenon that we still hear a lot about today - doctors in the spirit world who are still practising their skills.

George, from Surbiton, had suffered from a painful hernia for two years, but was reluctant to accept the verdict of his doctors that he needed an operation. Intrigued by an item in a 'psychic' newspaper offering sessions with spiritual healers, he went along.

First, the spirit doctor, through a medium, examined George 'mentally', and then asked what the 'earth people' were doing. Not a lot, in George's view, as he'd already been in pain for a couple of years. Assuring him that his wait was over, two assistants laid their hands on him. Initially, contact with the affected area made him yelp with pain, but within 24 hours all discomfort had gone. He discarded his truss...

Nowadays, alternative health centres are springing up in Kingston. Perhaps a bit of 'magic', in the form of tender loving care, still helps the medicine go down.

In Union Street, by the Gardens of Remembrance, there is a small Tudor-style building that is currently a baker's selling Danish pastries. It used to be the town mortuary. At the turn of the century, a popular pastime was fishing corpses out of the Thames. But the bodies brought out on the Kingston side earned the 'fishermen' a mere 2/6 (12 1/2p), so the more fiendish enthusiasts would push the body to the Teddington side, where the fee was 7/6 (37 1/2p). Delighting the young children who had gathered to watch, the bodies were hauled off to the mortuary in a ghoulish police ambulance - a handcart draped in a hooded black cloth.

A COUPLE OF UFO SIGHTINGS

Warminster might be *the* place for UFO sightings, but Kingston doesn't fare too badly...

We have a couple of reports: the first comes from the *Surrey Comet*, 17 June 1972. Sharon Dean (pseudonym), from Roehampton, was looking out over Richmond Park when she saw no fewer than *seven* UFOs coming in to land. Unfortunately, her parents were the only other witnesses. The first object, seen at about 10 o'clock in the evening, appeared as a 'conglomeration of lights', hovering about thirty feet above the ground.

After moving across the Park, the lights disappeared. Later, between 10pm and 12.15 am, Sharon saw a number of other lights converging on the same spot. They were a brilliant orange colour, but appeared to become duller as they landed. Sharon claims she could see a distinct flying-saucer shape to the objects.

What Sharon and her parents actually saw remains a mystery; a Richmond Park superintendent claimed that he knew of nothing out of the ordinary that had taken place that night. But the reported 'landing' makes this story interesting; we'd like to know more.

A first-hand account comes from John Chalcraft, the steward from Hampton Court. In about 1980, he was travelling to work on a single-decker bus at 7.30 am. Somewhere between Kingston and Hampton, he noticed through the window a sort of flying object, resembling a 'very smooth cylinder with rounded ends', hovering in the sky. It seemed to be made of stainless steel, but was 'quite definitely' not an aeroplane or an airship. It appeared to be stationary, but at one point seemed to start moving. A bit stunned by what he saw, John didn't think of asking the other three passengers on the bus if they, too, were witnessing the same thing.

John heard later that someone else *had* seen the mysterious object; there was a report, but no explanation, in the *Surrey Comet*. In his mind's eye, John can still see the 'UFO' quite vividly.

> Strolling through Richmond Park, can you be sure that the people in front of you are real? Whenever Mrs Bassett (pseudonym) was unable to walk her dog because of her irregular working hours, a kindly neighbour, an elderly gentleman, would offer to help out. Sadly, he died. A few weeks later, Mrs Bassett was walking her dog in Richmond Park. She noticed a bent figure walking ahead of her. His clothes and appearance strongly reminded Mrs Bassett of her former neighbour. The dog, anxious to greet her old friend, excitedly strained at the leash. Just as Mrs Bassett and the dog had nearly caught up with the stranger, he seemed to disappear into a nearby copse. They looked everywhere, but he was nowhere to be seen.

THE KINGSTON ZODIAC

When our family lived in North Kingston, we used to pass a flock of cooing doves housed in a front garden in Burton Road. It was a delightful local landmark; we wondered how the owner came to take up his unusual hobby. Perhaps he was simply responding to the pull of the stars? It so happens there's another dovecote in nearby Park Road. According to Mary Caine's book *The Kingston Zodiac*, the town is under the influence of Libra. This sign is often symbolised by the scales of justice but here, according to Mary, it is represented by an older symbol, the dove.

The dove is at the heart of Kingston and forms the centre of the zodiac. Mary asks: 'Is its beak the wedge-shaped market, grasping the Coronation Stone, its eye the parish church?' Other birds vie for attention: Cranes Wharf, Eagle Wharf, Raven's Ait, Hawks Road and the Kingfisher Centre. As a reminder of the Libran scales, the Law Courts are here too.

Mary argues that this terrestrial zodiac spans twelve miles across the outlying area. It is strikingly similar to the Glastonbury Zodiac discovered by Katharine Maltwood in 1935. Ms Maltwood called her discovery 'The Temple of Stars' because her circle of effigies corresponded to the constellations. She also claimed her circle as the original Round Table in Avalon, with Arthur and his chief knights seated around it as the zodiac signs.

Nearly fifty years later, Mary began studying a map of Kingston and, one by one, the twelve zodiac signs emerged. A thirteenth sign, the Dog of Langport, appeared to stand guard as far west as Chobham Common. Each sign was delineated by natural streams, tracks and boundaries and uncannily completed by roads, place names and folklore.

As with the Glastonbury Zodiac, flamboyant Leo the lion was first to hit the spotlight. The King of Beasts rules Chessington and has several royal residences. Hampton Court and Claremont House (former seat of King Leopold) are in the area; Nonsuch Palace was once near his tail. Mary considers that Hook on his collar suggests Leo is tethered: the lion chained to a rock occurs in Arthurian legend. There are real lions at the World of Adventures which is on the way to Leatherhead (once known as *Leo*dridan).

However fanciful the theory, Mary feels that the evidence is readily available. After all, astrologers find that the stars can influence an individual's character and destiny. Star temples suggest that this influence can also affect our environment. As Katharine Maltwood said: 'It is as if the stars had kissed the earth leaving their imprint'.

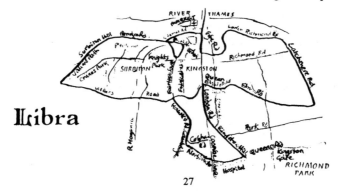

Libra

THE CORONATION STONE - A MAGICAL OBJECT?

One of Kingston's cherished traditions is that seven Anglo-Saxon kings were crowned here. The Coronation Stone, situated in a shady corner by the Guildhall, under the watchful eye of the police in the nearby station, is the town's most prized possession.

But we know surprisingly little about it. It's a weighty slab of grey sarsen sandstone, similar to the type of stone used in the construction of Stonehenge. But *who* brought it to Kingston, and how and when it got there, nobody knows. In fact, very little at all is known about the Stone's chequered history before the late 18th century. (A reference by map-maker John Speed in 1627 to the 'Chair of Majesty' seems unlikely to refer to the treasured artefact.) The Stone's possible value as a historical relic wasn't recognised until as late as the 1850's.

What we *do* know is that it didn't give its name to Kingston, which people tend to find surprising and even mildly disappointing. The town's name actually derives from 'Cyningestun', meaning the King's Estate. It was first mentioned in an ecclesiastical document of 838 that related to a council presided over by King Egbert - nearly 40 years *before* the first king was crowned in Kingston.

The other big question is - *why* was Kingston chosen for these hallowed ceremonies? One theory is that Kingston was once regarded as a special, sacred area. But the actual location of the town offers a more probable - if more mundane - explanation. The kingdom of Mercia was situated just north of the Thames; Kingston, an important town in Wessex, was well-placed strategically to unite the two regions.

But whatever the historical conjectures, there's no doubt about the Stone's fascination for both Kingstonians and visitors. It's much more than a mere chunk of stone, of symbolic interest only. It even seems to be regarded as a rather magical artefact, rather like the altar of the Roman Goddess of Fortuna (now in the Museum) on which coins used to be placed 'for luck', or for a safe journey. We're still just as superstitious. Visit the Stone on a busy, summer's day and you could well see a few coins scattered around.

Some regard the Stone as an object of power and influence. Recently, a couple of foreign visitors were seen dowsing the Stone with a pendulum, which was swinging to and fro quite vigorously. Curiosity got the better of a bystander, who asked what they were doing.

The gentleman explained that he and his wife had come to Kingston especially to dowse the Stone. In his opinion, it was as powerful as the Stone of Scone in Westminster Abbey, which they had also dowsed. It should, he said, give power to anyone who was crowned on it. He added: 'In the past, people understood things like that'.

The incident reminded us of a friend who had dowsed the Stone with divining rods a few years earlier. She, too, spoke of 'a good deal of power rising upwards from the Stone'.

So how powerful *were* the kings crowned on the Stone?

CURIOUS TALES OF KINGSTON'S KINGS

Edward, the first to be crowned in Kingston, in 900 AD, was undoubtedly a powerful king. The son of King Alfred (of 'cakes' fame), he managed for the first time to unite England as a single kingdom. But some of the kings who followed him were very young when they were crowned - and their reigns were sometimes cut short, often unceremoniously, before they'd had a chance to prove themselves. Today, it seems to be the stranger, more off-beat aspects of their lives that we remember.

Edwig's, for example. He was crowned in 956, when he was about 17. Right from the start, his heart wasn't really in it. He enjoyed 'the caresses of loose women'. (*Plus ça change...*) Indeed, so anxious was he for their company that he couldn't even wait for the Coronation banquet to end before slipping away to make merry in the preferred way.

St Dunstan the Abbot was, not surprisingly, alarmed by this unseemly behaviour, and fell out with the new king. After Edwig's death, St Dunstan dreamed he was carried away by devils. But, by the intervention of the Abbot's prayers, Edwig's doomed soul was saved.

The strangest myths surround Edward the Martyr, crowned in 975. Edward never had much luck. In 977, many of his closest advisers died. They fell through the floor during a meeting. The indomitable St. Dunstan was saved; he found himself marooned on a cross-beam whilst the 'badly-built' floors just disappeared from view.

A couple of years later, Edward was murdered. He was visiting his step-mother Aelfthryth and half-brother Ethelred. Just as Edward was accepting a glass of wine, Aelfthryth stabbed him. Nothing should stop her own son, Ethelred, from becoming king.

Legend has it that before Edward's body was placed in a tomb, it was hidden in a well that gradually became surrounded by a mysterious, glowing light. Soon, stories of miracles taking place at his tomb began to spread. Until Henry VIII ordered the dissolution of the monasteries in 1538, pilgrims flocked to Shaftesbury Abbey to visit his shrine. *The Anglo-Saxon Chronicle* stated that God would make sure his bones were sanctified.

Sanctified they *may* be, but there's an unholy squabble going on at the moment about the ownership of his bones. After a spell in the vaults of the Midland Bank (in a 'cutlery box') they are now in the care of the Russian Orthodox Church. Housed in a disused mortuary near Woking, they are on display to the public twice a year.

A strangely prophetic phenomenon occurred shortly after the crowning of Ethelred, Edward's successor, in 979. The *Chronicle* reports that 'In the same year was seen often-times a bloody cloud, in the likeness of fire; and that was most apparent at midnight; and was coloured in various ways. It was formed into manifold beams; then when it was about to dawn, it glided away'. The Danes invaded, and there was fire and bloodshed on an unprecedented scale.

To crown it all, there's even a suggestion that a cottage in Wargrave, Berkshire, once named 'Queen Emma's Cottage', is haunted by Queen Emma, Ethelred's wife.

AN EERIE ENCOUNTER ON THE PORTSMOUTH ROAD

One night Al and a friend were driving to Kingston along the Portsmouth Road. As they approached Esher, Al noticed a number of dips in the road and then unexpectedly felt very cold. His friend commented on the sudden chill. The temperature gauge registered a sharp drop.

'Everything clouded up and in the distance I saw a figure of a woman dressed all in white with long dark hair. She was standing in front of the car about fifty feet away, just hovering there'. Al went on to describe her modern appearance which he guessed to be roughly eighties' style. 'She was very pale and her dress was long with buttons down the front. Oh, and she had no shoes.

'Anyway, we drove straight through her! We both saw it, we looked at each other, we knew we'd both seen it and we thought, well, bloody hell!' About three weeks later, Al and his friend were driving along the same stretch of road at night when the temperature dropped again. Both anticipated another sighting of the figure but nothing appeared.

A year went by before Al and his friend were to find themselves travelling along the same route at night. This time they were accompanied by Al's new girlfriend; they both enjoyed telling her of their previous experiences. She dismissed the tale scornfully. They came to the series of dips. Everyone noticed the sudden change of atmosphere, again confirmed by the temperature gauge. Al is now resigned to it: 'Every time we go down that part of the road the temperature drops'.

Al's story reminded us of an incident that happened to our family some years ago. We were travelling along the same stretch of road at about midnight. The car slowly ground to a halt, the electrics having inexplicably died on us. We were left stranded in pitch blackness, in the middle of Esher Common, until help arrived.

It is refreshing to come across a White Lady in modern dress. But the mystery remains: who is she, and what happened to her on that lonely stretch of road one dark night? We hope that she wasn't another hapless motorist - who was less fortunate than we were.

IS THERE ANYBODY STILL THERE?

There are a number of reports from some years ago; we went in search of new witnesses...

H Samuel

H Samuel, the jewellers, has been cleverly restored to its original 17th century appearance on the corner of Church Street in the Market Place. In the 1980s, when the site was occupied by their old rival, Ratner's, there were frequent reports that things weren't quite right...

Duncan Thomas (pseudonym) was manager at the time and his suspicions were aroused soon after taking over the shop. The burglar alarms kept ringing at all hours during weekends - then switching themselves off again. The system was found to be in perfect working order.

On one occasion, the family dog tore down the stairs as if, according to Duncan, 'the devil himself was behind him'. Sales staff only ventured upstairs in pairs and complained of a 'presence' watching them. Once a row of pendulum clocks, usually stopped last thing before closing, were found ticking away next morning, all showing the same time.

Who *is* the ghost who still enjoys wreaking a bit of havoc? It's anyone's guess.

A Disgruntled Ale-wife

Dipping into the archives, the most voluble character we came across in the building's history, and the one most likely to cling tenaciously to former haunts, is an 18th century ale-wife who brewed her ales on the premises when 'Samuel' was the Old Queen's Head.

In those days, woe betide brewers if their ales didn't come up to scratch. When the inspectors turned up, the best bet was probably to go along with them, smiling sweetly and vowing to do better next time. But that wasn't the ale-wife's style at all. She ranted and raged at her tormentors for daring to pass judgement on her brewing abilities...

Not a wise move. Until the end of the 18th century, 'scolds' were rewarded with an ignominious punishment - a ducking (sometimes prolonged) in the Hogsmill River. Think of the humiliation of this proud woman as she was unceremoniously wheeled through the Market Place to Clattern Bridge on the ducking stool and dunked, like a ginger nut, into the river. Reports say that she then pounced on her attackers, and nearly received a second ducking 'before she was dry from the first'!

We'd like to think that the spirit of the ale-wife is still hovering at H Samuel, standing up for our rights. In her coffin she *may* be, but she was clearly not a woman to take things lying down...

Once, the area around H Samuel was a lively and colourful corner of the Market Place. Nowadays, the most intemperate activity that takes place is Daisy Ann selling flowers from her stall. But rumour has it that, last century, opposite the Old Queen's Head and next to a pig sty, *wives* were sold. We haven't found a local account, but an item that appeared in the *Maidstone Journal* in 1847 helps put us in the picture. (Maidstone was comparable to Kingston in several ways.) A wife was led into the Market with a halter around her neck. She and her two children were sold for a total sum of 10/- (50p). But these sales seemed to be an unusual event, and not everyone approved of them. Indeed, the seller in this case died 5 weeks later - from an aneurism of the aorta, it was said. Or, as gleefully reported by the local paper, by 'visitation from God'.

Office

Sam Khan (pseudonym), manager of the Harry Fenton menswear shop in 1980, claimed the previous manager lasted only a few minutes in the job. Sam could understand why. He, too, felt uneasy being in the shop on his own and often sensed an unseen 'someone' when working at his desk.

Upstairs, a feeling of menace chilled the atmosphere. The attic rooms had been left abandoned for many years; squeaking mice cavorted amongst the dusty cobwebs. But one room, no one dared enter at all; even the spiders scuttled away in fear.

Window dressers were reluctant to come to the branch as dummies would unexpectedly fly out at them. The building was exorcised and the strange phenomena quietened down. But they were still not silent. One day Sam heard a loud bang: a door, left open, had slammed shut. He opened it and, a few moments later, it slammed again. Rooted to the spot, Sam watched it in the mirror. There was no draught, and no obvious explanation.

Today, the premises are occupied by Office, a bright and trendy shoe shop. A young assistant told us of the rumour that a man had once hanged himself upstairs - in the eerie attic room. So far, he has nothing out of the ordinary to report, but local interest continues. Recently, a party of school children and their teacher gathered outside - on the off chance of catching the shoes dancing in the window perhaps?

Beatties

Unnerving activities in Beatties model shop in Eden Street were so alarming that exorcism rites had to be carried out on the premises for some months.

The manager, Mike Higgins, explained why to the *Kingston Borough News* in 1980. Philip Mann, his assistant, was becoming unduly sensitive to much of the unusual phenomena. On several occasions, he stayed behind after closing time and felt the sensation of a 'presence'. Once he saw a figure walking right through the shop. It was a woman dressed in Saxon clothing, 'surrounded by mist as though she was on the river'.

Other members of staff reported a 'strange atmosphere'. One had felt an icy touch on her arm, and two others reported independently that they had suddenly felt very cold. They were all very relieved when the attempts at exorcism seemed successful.

Checking up on the local history, Philip found that the shop occupied the site of the old Hodgson's Brewery in Heathen Street - Eden Street's old name. The brewery had a reputation for being haunted but we have found no stories which relate to this period.

Sixteen years later, we were curious to find out if there has been any further activity. The manager, Dean Scott, told us that the previous manager had confided in him. Arriving first thing in the morning, he said, boxes used to fall off their shelves across his path as he walked through the aisles. He heard occasional noises which he couldn't identify.

Today, things are pretty quiet although the manager did mention a rumour that the shop may stand on an old swimming pool long since forgotten. There is a convincing slope to the floor in the basement to support the idea. Could this conjecture tie up with the theory of Roman baths in Denmark Road? Indeed, could the spirit of the Saxon maid not be bathed in river mist but *steam* from a Roman hot spring? (All names have been changed)

Bradford & Bingley

No. 1 Thames Street has a history dating back to medieval days and retains the timber frames from the time it was rebuilt during the reign of Elizabeth I. Now, with a beautifully restored interior, it is occupied by the Bradford & Bingley Building Society.

It is alleged that one of Henry VIII's many fancy women would consort with him here.

One can imagine Henry taking a boat from Hampton Court to Kingston and darting from the landing stage into King's Alley. Perhaps he would then steal into the house under cover of darkness and enjoy an illicit rendezvous with his ladylove. True to form, when fear of the discovery threatened scandal, it is said Henry had the woman murdered.

Rumour says that her hapless spirit still haunts the premises. Unfortunately, helpful though the members of staff were, they could offer us no information on recent sightings.

But oddly enough, the story has a ring of truth. Legend has it that there's a tunnel, wide enough to accommodate a carriage, from Hampton Court Palace; it runs under the Thames, and emerges in the basement of the old Cardinal's Store - just a few doors down from the Bradford & Bingley. It's said that Henry VIII had the tunnel built to make it easier to carry on his nocturnal assignations with lady friends. More private than boats.

Could Henry VIII have been an early Chunneller...?

Clark's Art Shop

When it comes to spine-chilling tales, the one about the former art shop, Clarks, takes - the booby prize. Not all tales of the supernatural make your hair stand on end: some have a definite 'Ahh!' factor. At one time, before the sharp bend in Eden Street was dominated by the huge back wall of BHS, there was a row of shops which included Clark's.

Sometimes, 'ghosts' appear to be so solid and ordinary that the only giveaway is their style of dress. Which is why a manager at Clarks felt a bit nervous when a little old lady turned up in the shop one day, wearing a bonnet and a long grey dress. When she vanished as soon as he offered assistance, he was even more bemused. Later, a gentleman of the same period visited the shop; he, too, suddenly and mysteriously disappeared. Thereafter, the two elderly people would appear together. It seems that the couple fits the description of two former managers of the shop who were very attached to the place. So attached that they couldn't keep away?

Recent developments have no doubt benefited Kingston enormously - but it's still nice to have the occasional reminder of the way things used to be...

'I'm sure it's around here *somewhere*'

34

BIBLIOGRAPHY

The Story of Kingston	June Sampson
Kingston Characters	June Sampson
The Book of Kingston	Shaan Butters
Kingston Then and Now	Margaret Bellars
The Kingston Zodiac	Mary Caine
The Book of Curses	Stuart Gordon
The Ghost Hunter's Guide	Peter Underwood
A Gazetteer of British Ghosts	Peter Underwood
Children of the Light	Jonathan Fryer
An Encyclopedia of Ghosts and Spirits	John and Anne Spencer
Hampton Court - a History	Philip Lindsay
Malden Old and New	Stephen Day
The Haunted South	Joan Forman
Old Kingston	W G Ayliffe
Tradition Magazine, 1992	various
Strange Berkshire	an ASSAP Publication
KTS Newsletter, February 1996	
The Anglo Saxon Chronicle	

AKNOWLEDGEMENTS

Many thanks to:-

Tim Eversen at the Local History Room
Ruth Murphy and Clive Whichelow
Winnie Stewart
Mary Caine
Mrs C Olney
Dawn Tomazou at the Mitre
John Chalcraft and the staff at Hampton Court
Al and Mike at the Plough
Don Walker and staff at the Home of Compassion
Russell family
Kingston Tourists Guides
The staff at All Saints' Church
All the long-suffering bar staff, shop assistants and members of the public who fielded our strange questions so admirably!